D1056484

MIDDLE AGES

Troll Associates

MIDDLE AGES

by Louis Sabin

Illustrated by Hal Frenck

Troll Associates

Library of Congress Cataloging in Publication Data

Sabin, Louis.
Middle Ages.

Summary: Briefly describes conditions of life for noblemen, monks, priests, peasants, pilgrims, tradesmen, and others during the Middle Ages in Europe.
1. Middle Ages—History—Juvenile literature. 2. Europe—History—476-1492—Juvenile literature. [1. Middle Ages. 2. Europe—History—476-1492. 3. Civilization, Medieval] I. Frenck, Hal, ill. II. Title.
D118.S26 1984 940.1 84-2670
ISBN 0-8167-0174-1 (lib. bdg.)
ISBN 0-8167-0175-X (pbk.)

Printed in the United States of America

10 9 8 7 6 5 4 3 2 1

Hoofbeats thunder across the fields as knights in shining armor charge toward one another, their lances pointing toward their adversaries. Lords and their ladies feast on delicious foods at lavish banquet tables inside great stone castles. Poor peasants labor endlessly in the fields outside the manor walls, struggling to support not only themselves, but their wealthy landowners as well.

This is life in the Middle Ages.

The Middle Ages lasted roughly 1,000 years, from about A.D. 500 to about A.D. 1500. They began after the fall of the powerful Roman Empire and ended at the beginning of the age of strong national governments.

When scholars refer to the Middle Ages, they are talking about the history of only a very small part of the world. That part is Western Europe, which extends from the Scandinavian countries in the north to Great Britain in the west to Italy in the south and to Germany's Rhine River in the east.

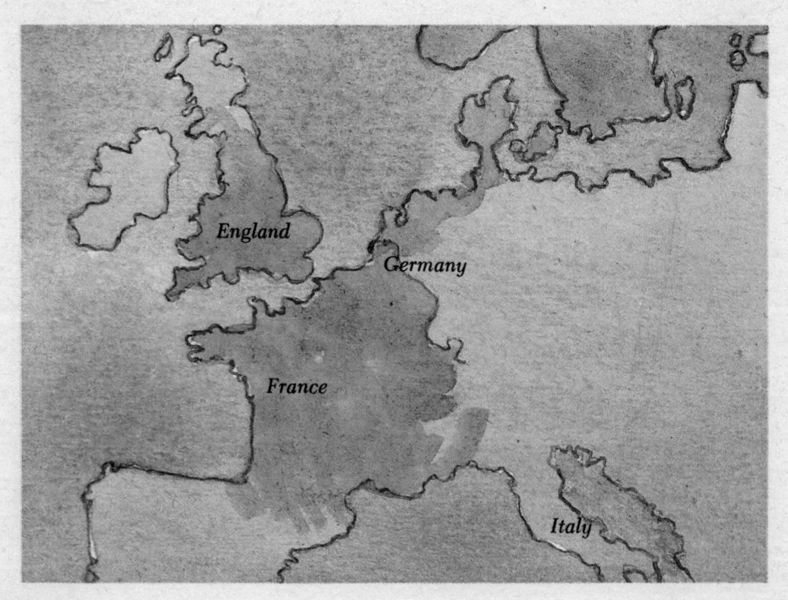

While Western Europe was struggling through the Middle Ages, there were advanced civilizations thriving in India, China, the Moslem Middle East, and parts of Africa. But the Middle Ages is a period of particular interest to us because our culture is primarily based on the history of Western Europe.

In ancient times, at the height of its power, the Roman Empire controlled almost all of Europe, the Middle East, and the northern coast of Africa. Then, slowly, the Empire weakened.

The Roman government suffered from corruption. Warlike barbarian tribes defeated the Roman armies. Finally the Roman Empire fell, and Western Europe was thrown into chaos. There was no longer an Empire with a strong army to protect people. The only security was in manorialism, and later, feudalism.

Manorialism was a way of life that centered on the manor. A manor was an estate, owned by a landlord or lord. Sometimes a manor was surrounded by a high wall. There were farm lands, pastures for raising cattle and sheep, huts for the

peasants who worked on the estate, and a manor house for the lord and his family.

The manor house was sometimes a castle of stone. But sometimes it was a wooden building not much bigger or better than the peasants' huts.

The peasants who worked the land were protected by the lords. But they paid for this protection by being virtual slaves of the manor. By law, they could not leave the land. And they belonged to their master from the day they were born until the day they died.

Every manor had to produce everything the people needed. A wealthy manor usually had a number of people with different skills. There would be a blacksmith, a baker, a miller to grind the grain, a carpenter, a barber, a shoemaker, and other craftsmen.

There was little trade and little travel—at least in the early Middle Ages. Robbers, highwaymen, and cutthroats were everywhere. It wasn't safe to travel or to carry goods from one area to another.

Feudalism developed later in the Middle Ages. The feudal system was a network of lords and vassals. Vassals were noblemen who pledged their loyalty to a lord. In return, that lord gave each vassal an estate or *fief* to rule. As rulers of fiefs, these noblemen were also lords, who had vassals of their own. Those vassals pledged their loyalty in exchange for smaller fiefs, which they ruled.

Under the feudal system, warfare often broke out between different lords. Then armies of knights in heavy armor battled against one another. When they were not actually fighting, the knights practiced their wartime skills by holding jousting tournaments.

Culture and learning might have died completely in Western Europe if it had not been for the church. Literature and learning were kept alive in the monasteries. Monks created magnificently illustrated books and scrolls. Priests taught reading and writing. But few people in the Middle Ages felt the need for such intellectual skills.

The church was also the only unifying force in Europe. The lord of the manor—as well as the peasants—obeyed the laws of the church. Any lord who broke church law could be excommunicated, or denied the benefits of church membership. In addition, all the people on his manor could also be denied the benefits of the church. Understandably, few lords were willing to defy the church.

Religious faith dominated every aspect of life in the Middle Ages. For most people, life was short, hard, and poor. The only hope they had was the afterlife promised by the church. And so, worship grew very intense.

As this religious fervor grew, people began to make pilgrimages. A pilgrimage was a trip to a religious shrine or holy place. As more and more people made pilgrimages, a change came over Western Europe. Small towns slowly developed around the shrines.

Pilgrims needed places to sleep and food to eat. Inns were established to meet those needs. Small shops began to appear near the inns, offering the services of tailors, shoemakers, and barbers. Gradually, these groups of shops became towns.

The same religious faith that prompted people to make pilgrimages brought about

the Crusades. The Crusades were Christian military expeditions. The Christians wanted to recapture the Holy Land from the Moslems. For about 200 years—from the end of the eleventh century to the end of the thirteenth century—thousands of crusaders moved across Europe.

Most of the crusaders were members of private armies led by kings or powerful nobles. The armies were accompanied by peasants who had to do the cooking, care for their animals, repair armor, and do other forms of work. As these large groups traveled over Europe, they brought more changes. Trade and communication—which had died out with the fall of the Roman Empire—were revived during the Crusades.

However, the Crusades never accomplished their original goal. Most of the crusaders didn't even reach the Holy Land. Many died on the way. Some settled down in different parts of Europe. And others simply gave up and turned back for home.

Some of the towns where crusading groups stopped grew into cities. They became centers of trade and commerce. Great cathedrals were built. Art and architecture thrived. Chivalry—the code of proper behavior for a knight—turned crude warriors into civilized people.

As city life returned to Europe, the middle class grew stronger. At the same time, the feudal system grew weaker. But it was a slow process.

Then a terrible epidemic swept across Europe. Called the plague, or the Black Death, it brought rapid, far-reaching changes. The plague struck in Italy, France, Great Britain—in fact, all over Europe. Within three years, more than one fourth of the entire population of Europe was wiped out.

The plague killed nobles and peasants alike. It turned thriving manors into empty castles and untended fields. The Black Death brought death to the feudal economy.

Those who were lucky enough to survive the plague and who had skills were in great demand. A blacksmith could get a good price for his skills, as could a baker, a weaver, a cobbler, or any other skilled craftsman. The nobles, without their large private armies and hordes of peasant laborers, became more dependent upon their kings.

The power of the kings increased as the power of the nobles lessened. Nations began to take shape. As they became more and more powerful, the kings came into conflict with the church. Even the threat of excommunication did not stop some of them. A new national awareness was growing, and people no longer felt that they should be ruled by the pope in Rome.

This was a time of new ideas. As religion loosened its grip, the people turned to more worldly interests. Music, painting, architecture, and the other arts were no longer devoted solely to the glorification of the church. Palaces and grand homes were built instead of cathedrals.

Instead of church music, composers wrote music to please their royal masters. Even Latin, the language of the church, began to be replaced by English, French, Spanish, and other national tongues. And as these national identities flourished and more and more new ideas took hold, the Middle Ages came to a close.